PREDATOR PROFILES

TIGERS
– BUILT FOR THE HUNT –

by Julia Vogel

Consultant: Dr. Jackie Gai, DVM
Wildlife Veterinarian

CAPSTONE PRESS
a capstone imprint

First Facts are published by Capstone Press,
1710 Roe Crest Drive, North Mankato, Minnesota 56003
www.capstonepub.com

Library of Congress Cataloging-in-Publication Data
Vogel, Julia, author.
  Tigers : built for the hunt / by Julia Vogel.
    pages cm. — (First facts. Predator profiles)
  Summary: "Informative, engaging text and vivid photos introduce readers
to the predatory lives of tigers"—Provided by publisher.
  Audience: Ages 6-9
  Audience: K to grade 3
  ISBN 978-1-4914-5036-9 (library binding)
  ISBN 978-1-4914-5080-2 (eBook PDF)
1. Tiger—Juvenile literature. 2. Predation (Biology)—Juvenile literature. I. Title.
  QL737.C23V646 2016
  599.756—dc23   2015006663

Editorial Credits
Brenda Haugen, editor; Juliette Peters, designer;
Tracy Cummins, media researcher; Katy LaVigne, production specialist

Photo Credits
FLPA: Gerard Lacz, 15; Getty Images: Andy Rouse, 9, Steve Winter, 13; Shutterstock: Anan
Kaewkhammul, 2, Design Element, Anne-Marie B, Cover, Arangan Ananth, 7, Colette3, 5,
Back Cover, Erika Kusuma Wardani, 16, Jean-Edouard Rozey, 3, Julian W, 19, Matthew Cole,
14, Michal Ninger, 4, Nachiketa Bajaj, 17, pashabo, Design Element, Sarah Cheriton-Jones,
12, Vaclav Volrab, 6, Volodymyr Burdiak, 10; Thinkstock: davemhuntphotography, 21, Fuse,
11, Martin Bornack, 18, ShinOkamoto, 1.

Printed in China by Nordica
0415/CA21500544
042015   008845NORDF15

TABLE OF CONTENTS

BIG, STRONG CAT

A tiger quietly slips through the jungle. The hungry cat is searching for **prey**. Like other cats, tigers are **predators** that only eat meat. They hunt many kinds of prey, such as moose, deer, and wild pigs.

The biggest tigers weigh 660 pounds (300 kilograms). They can kill a water buffalo twice their size.

prey—an animal hunted by another animal for food

predator—an animal that hunts other animals for food

NIGHT HUNTER

Tigers hunt at night. The cats' **keen** eyes see six times better in darkness than people's eyes can.

Sharp hearing also helps tigers at night. A twig's snap gets a tiger's attention. Is it a wild pig, a deer, or some other prey? The hunt is on!

FACT

Unlike other cats, tigers seem to like water. They swim to catch deer, crocodiles, and other prey.

keen—the ability to notice things easily

THE NOSE KNOWS

Tigers do not rely much on their sense of smell to find prey. But their sense of smell is still important. It helps tigers know where to hunt. Each tiger leaves droppings and rubs against trees to mark its hunting **territory**. These **scent marks** warn other tigers to stay away.

FACT

The size of a tiger's territory depends on how many prey animals live there. Jungles rich in wildlife can feed more tigers.

territory—an area of land that an animal claims as its own to live in

scent mark—a smell to warn other animals to stay away

HIDDEN HUNTER

A tiger can run fast but not very far. Some prey animals, such as antelopes, can outrun a tiger in a long chase. Instead of chasing prey, a tiger **stalks** its meal. Its padded paws help it move in silence.

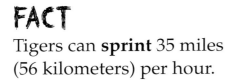

FACT
Tigers can **sprint** 35 miles (56 kilometers) per hour.

stalk—to hunt an animal in a secret, quiet way

sprint—to run fast for a short distance

A tiger hides and waits to catch prey by surprise. In thick brush, a tiger's orange and black fur gives it **camouflage**. Prey cannot spot its hidden enemy. The prey steps closer. The hungry tiger waits. At last, the prey moves within reach.

FACT

Each tiger has its own pattern of stripes. The pattern is as unique as a person's fingerprint. No two people have the same fingerprints.

camouflage—a pattern or color on an animal's skin or fur that makes it blend in with the things around it

The tiger leaps! Its huge body slams down the prey. The tiger's sharp claws hold on tight. Its long **canine** teeth bite deep into the prey's neck. The tiger's powerful jaws crush the animal's bones.

A tiger can eat 66 pounds (30 kg) of meat in one meal. A tiger may feed on a big kill for four days and not eat again for two weeks.

FACT

To keep their claws sharp, tigers tuck them inside their paws when not in use.

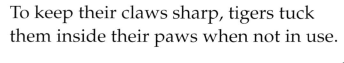

canine—a long, pointed tooth

LEARNING TO HUNT

Like other **mammals**, female tigers make milk for their young. The 3-pound (1.4-kg) newborns drink milk for up to three months. Then the mother brings them meat. When the cubs are 6 months old, they follow their mother on their first hunt.

At first cubs watch their mother. She teaches them how to stalk, wait, and kill.

mammal—a warm-blooded animal that breathes air; mammals have hair or fur; female mammals feed milk to their young

Cubs also learn to hunt by playing together. Playing builds muscles to run and pounce. Later they practice killing small animals, such as **piglets** and **fawns**. Cubs stay with their mothers until they can catch enough food to survive.

piglet—a young pig

fawn—a young deer

YOUNG PREDATORS

By age 2 cubs are grown. Young adult females find territories close to their mothers. Young males often wander far away. Each tiger is a powerful predator, ready to hunt on its own.

FACT
Although adult tigers live alone, they sometimes share a kill with other tigers that live nearby.

AMAZING BUT TRUE!

Tigers have the largest canine teeth of all big cats. These teeth can be as long as an adult person's finger! A tiger's canines are strong too. They won't break even when a tiger bites through thick bones.

GLOSSARY

camouflage (KA-muh-flahzh)—a pattern or color on an animal's skin or fur that makes it blend in with the things around it

canine (KAY-nyn)—a long, pointed tooth

fawn (FAWN)—a young deer

keen (KEEN)—the ability to notice things easily

mammal (MAM-uhl)—a warm-blooded animal that breathes air; mammals have hair or fur; female mammals feed milk to their young

piglet (PIG-let)—a young pig

predator (PRED-uh-tur)—an animal that hunts other animals for food

prey (PRAY)—an animal hunted by another animal for food

scent mark (SENT MARK)—a smell to warn other animals to stay away

sprint (SPRINT)—to run fast for a short distance

stalk (STAWK)—to hunt an animal in a secret, quiet way

territory (TER-uh-tor-ee)—an area of land that an animal claims as its own to live in

READ MORE

Franchino, Vicky. *Tigers.* Nature's Children. New York: Children's Press, 2012.

Marsh, Laura F. *Tigers.* National Geographic Kids. Washington, D.C.: National Geographic, 2012.

Murray, Julie. *Tigers.* Asian Animals. Minneapolis: ABDO Publishing, Company, 2013.

INTERNET SITES

FactHound offers a safe, fun way to find Internet sites related to this book. All of the sites on FactHound have been researched by our staff.

Here's all you do:

Visit *www.facthound.com*

Type in this code: 9781491450369

Super-cool stuff!

Check out projects, games and lots more at
www.capstonekids.com

CRITICAL THINKING USING THE COMMON CORE

1. How do tiger cubs learn to hunt?
   (Key Ideas and Details)

2. What is a territory? What do you think the tiger
   is doing on page 9? (Craft and Structure)

INDEX